Living by Rivers

Neil Morris

FRANKLIN WATTS

LONDON • SYDNEY

An Appleseed Editions book

First published in 2004 by Franklin Watts
96 Leonard Street, London, EC2A 4XD

Franklin Watts Australia
45–51 Huntley Street, Alexandria, NSW 2015

© 2004 Appleseed Editions

Created by Appleseed Editions Ltd,
Well House, Friars Hill, Guestling, East Sussex, TN35 4ET

Designed by Helen James

ISBN 0 7496 5831 2

A CIP catalogue for this book is available from the British Library.

Photographs by Corbis (AFP, Paul Almasy, Annie Griffiths Belt, Bettmann, Michael Busselle, Elio Ciol, Lee Cohen, Dean Conger, Keith Dannemiller, Edifice, Owen Franken, Philip Gould, Angelo Hornak, Jeremy Horner, Jaques Langevin, Richard List, London Aerial Photo Library, Kevin R. Morris, Tom Nebbia, Charles OíRear, Hans Georg Roth, Charles E. Rotkin, Royalty-Free, SHAFFER JIM/CORBIS SYGMA, Ted Spiegel, Stapleton Collection, Vince Streano, Tim Thompson, Patrick Ward, Julia Waterlow; Eye Ubiquitous, K.M. Westermann, Nik Wheeler, Staffan Widstrand, Adam Woolfitt, Michael S. Yamashita)

Printed in the USA

Contents

Introduction

Throughout history, people have chosen to live beside the world's rivers. Small settlements, towns and cities have grown up on riverbanks, allowing people to live close to a reliable source of fresh water. This was important for farmers, who needed water to help grow their **crops**. In earlier times, before there were railways, cars or surfaced roads, boats were a useful means of getting around. This meant that rivers became important transport routes. Later, large boats were also used to carry heavy **cargoes**, and special river **ports** developed. Today, many people make their home near a river simply because it is a pleasant place to live.

▲ *Many people enjoy spending family time on the banks of beautiful rivers.*

Where rivers come from

Most rivers start high up on hills and mountains, where rainfall collects and forms small streams. This beginning of a river is called its **source**. The streams flow downhill and eventually come together to make a river. This larger flow of water wears the land away and makes its own **channel**. Over many years the channel may get deeper and wider, forming a river valley. Rivers go on flowing until they reach the sea, at a place called the river's **mouth**.

When a river reaches flatter land, it gets wider and starts to loop around. This is a popular place for housing, but it can suffer from floods.

Crossing the river

Early people used logs, rafts and canoes to cross rivers. But as settlements got bigger, people wanted an easier way to get from one riverbank to the other. **Archaeologists** have discovered that there was a bridge across the Euphrates River, in the ancient city of Babylon, by the sixth century BC. They believe there might have been a bridge there much earlier than that. The ancient Chinese and Egyptians also built bridges of bricks and stone. Later, the ancient Romans became expert bridge-builders. In their capital of Rome, they built bridges across the river Tiber that are still standing today.

The famous Ponte Vecchio ('Old Bridge') was built across the river Arno in Florence, Italy, in 1345. Like many old city bridges, it was covered with buildings. They originally contained the shops of butchers, blacksmiths and leather-workers.

Early Settlement

Historians believe that modern humans – people like us – first appeared a very long time ago in Africa. About 100,000 years ago, groups of humans moved north into Asia and Europe. They were on the move for many thousands of years, until finally there were people living all over the world. As they travelled, these early people hunted wild animals and gathered fruit, berries and roots for food. Many of them travelled along the coasts as they moved, and others followed rivers inland. This meant that these hunter-gatherers were never far from life-giving fresh water. And the rivers contained another advantage – there were lots of fish to catch and eat.

▲ *The Khoikoin people of South Africa traditionally hunted and gathered near rivers. This picture was drawn by a European artist in the 19th century. It shows a Khoikoin settlement beside the Orange River.*

Between the rivers

About 8,000 years ago, people started to settle in a region of south-west Asia that lay between two great rivers – the Tigris and the Euphrates. The ancient Greeks later called this region Mesopotamia, meaning 'between the rivers'. Both rivers begin in the mountains of present-day Turkey, running south through Iraq before

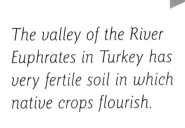
The valley of the River Euphrates in Turkey has very fertile soil in which native crops flourish.

coming together to flow into the Persian Gulf. In southern Mesopotamia, the **fertile** soil that was sometimes covered by the floodwaters of the two rivers was good for growing crops. Groups of hunter-gatherers decided to settle there and take up farming.

Givers of life

Ancient peoples developed their own forms of religion, worshipping the forces of nature that meant most to them. The people of Mesopotamia, who were later called Sumerians, had many gods and goddesses. One of the most important was Enki, the god of water, who was usually shown with streams of water spouting from his shoulders. Enki was worshipped as a creator god, whose rivers gave life to everyone. He was sometimes shown as half goat, half fish. The ancient Egyptians named their river god Hapi. He represented the River Nile when it was in flood. Hapi was usually portrayed as a fat man, to show that he was healthy and full of life.

This statue shows an ancient Sumerian goddess. She is pouring water to give life to fields near the Euphrates.

From Village to City

Ancient peoples such as the Sumerians settled beside rivers and learned how to grow crops. This meant that they no longer needed to move each year to find more food. As the population increased and people had more time for building, their settlements grew into villages full of mud-brick houses. Some villages grew into towns, and then into large cities full of monuments and impressive buildings. Ancient Sumer became part of the Babylonian Empire, with its capital at Babylon, on the River Euphrates. There King Nebuchadnezzar II found a new use for the river. He used it to water the Hanging Gardens of Babylon, which were built around 600 BC and became known as one of the Seven Wonders of the Ancient World.

Centres of civilization

Many ancient towns were founded near the mouth of a river, where people first arrived by sea. According to tradition, the city of Rome was

▲ *The water needed for the Hanging Gardens of Babylon may have been lifted from the river Euphrates by a chain of buckets. These were probably driven by slaves on a treadmill.*

founded on seven hills in 753 BC. It lies on the banks of the river Tiber, which flows for almost 400 kilometres from the Apennine Mountains to the Mediterranean Sea. Rome is just 16 kilometres from the sea, which made it an ideal location

Buda and Pest were originally two separate towns, on opposite banks of the Danube. They combined in 1873 to make the city of Budapest.

from which to build an empire. The Romans went on to build many more river cities throughout their empire, including Budapest (which they called 'Aquincum'), on the River Danube, in AD 100, and London (known as 'Londinium'), on the Thames, in AD 50.

River island

When the Romans arrived in what is now Paris in 52 BC, they found a small settlement on an island in the river Seine. A Gallic tribe known as the Parisii lived on the island, and they burned their houses rather than surrender them to the Romans. The Romans called the settlement Lutetia (meaning 'midwater dwelling'), but as the town spread out from the island to both banks of the river, it became known as Paris. Today the city has a population of more than nine million, but the original Seine island is still there. It is called Île de la Cité, and eight bridges link it to the riverbanks.

The cathedral of Notre-Dame ('Our Lady') stands on the island in the River Seine where the city of Paris began. Building of the cathedral began in 1163.

Getting Around

Many thousands of years ago, before proper roads were built, people used rivers to get around. Some hollowed tree trunks to make canoes. Others used **reeds** collected from riverbanks and marshes, pressing and weaving them together to make them watertight. Later, Native Americans and others made canoes from the bark of birch trees, while the Inuit of the Arctic used animal skins for their **kayaks**. All these riverboats were driven by the power of human muscles. In northern Europe, the Vikings used lightweight wooden riverboats, taking them out of the water and carrying them across **rapids**. Later, sails used the power of the wind, and in recent times coal, **diesel** and other fuels have made river travelling much easier.

Small boats called coracles were made of animal skins stretched over a wicker frame. They were traditionally used in Wales and Ireland, and Native Americans paddled a similar 'bullboat'.

Up and down the Nile

The ancient Egyptians used paddles to propel and steer their reed boats up and down the Nile. By about 3000 BC, they had added a square sail, which was useful for travelling upriver towards the south, because the wind normally blew that way. Travelling north, towards the Mediterranean Sea, was easy – they just drifted downstream with the flow of the river. Today, passengers travel along the Nile in a different way. Many visitors to Egypt sail between ancient sites, such as pyramids and temples, on cruise boats, which act as floating hotels. The locals, however, still use smaller craft to get around.

These boats with triangular sails are called feluccas. They are still used by Egyptians today, for carrying small cargoes as well as people.

Paddling and steaming

In 1807, an American boat named *Clermont* steamed for 240 kilometres up the Hudson River from New York to Albany. The river voyage took about 30 hours, and since railways did not yet exist, this way of travelling was a great success. Five years later, steamboats started carrying passengers up and down the Mississippi River. Steam drove a huge paddle at the **stern** of the boat, which pushed the craft along. Today, the famous Mississippi steamboats are still popular with tourists.

▼ *Launched in 1976, the* Mississippi Queen *is the world's largest riverboat. Its six decks offer luxury cabins.*

Barges and Canals

Barges are a river's equivalent of trucks on roads or goods trains on railways. They are used to carry heavy cargoes such as coal, grain and cement. Centuries ago, people or animals walked along a towpath beside the river, pulling barges along the river with ropes. Many modern barges are pulled or pushed along by small, powerful boats called tugs, or they have their own diesel engines. They are long and narrow in shape so that they can carry big loads but still pass each other on the river. During the **Industrial Revolution**, engineers began widening rivers and connecting them to **canals**. This meant that the new factories could deliver their goods to towns and ports more easily.

Some cities in the world are built on canals; because of this, canal boats are an important form of transport.

The Rhine and the Danube

The River Rhine is the busiest waterway in Europe. It begins in the Swiss Alps and flows for 1,320 kilometres through Germany and the Netherlands to the North Sea. It forms a natural link between the main industrial region of Germany and the huge port of Rotterdam. One of the Rhine's **tributaries**, the Main, is connected by a canal to the River Danube (which flows 2,860 kilometres from Germany's Black Forest to the Black Sea). When the Main-Danube Canal opened in 1992, boats were able to travel all the way from the Black Sea to the North Sea.

River cities often use barges to transport their goods to other places where they can be sold. Pictured here is a barge on the River Rhine at St. Goar, Germany.

The Panama Canal

The Panama Canal is only 82 kilometres long, but it is one of the most famous waterways in the world. This is because it links the Atlantic and Pacific Oceans across Central America, saving ships a long voyage around the tip of South America. The canal was built by the United States and completed in 1914. On December 31, 1999, control of the canal was given back to Panama. It is very important to this small country (which is less than 1/100th the size of the US) and its people. On average, 37 ships pass through the canal every day, though it is too narrow for the world's biggest ships. Parts of the canal are being widened, providing work for many Panamanians.

*The Panama Canal lies slightly above sea level, so ships have to pass through locks on their way into and out of the canal. The **locks** raise or lower ships by letting water in or out.*

Traditional Houses

People who live beside rivers soon learn that waterways often change course, and that the level of water changes with the seasons. In the Amazon rainforest of South America, some fishing people – such as the Mura of western Brazil – spend most of their time in their canoes, where they feel comfortable and safe. The Warrau people of Venezuela live in small thatched huts near rivers, but those in very wet areas build their village on a platform of logs covered with clay. At the Amazon port of Iquitos, in Peru, some people live in floating log-raft houses. These are similar to the houseboats that you can still see in cities such as London. These flat-bottomed boats stay moored, or secured, on the riverbank, and their owners have **gangplanks** leading up to their front doors.

Living on stilts

Many river people around the world raise their houses above the ground – or above the river itself – on stilts. Stilt houses are very common in south-east Asia. When the river is low and the ground dry, people often keep their animals and supplies under their houses. In Malaysia and Thailand, the stilts are usually made of bamboo. In eastern Malaysia, the Iban and Bidayuh people

▲ *Houseboats on the River Thames, in London. These dwellings are very comfortable and have most of the modern conveniences of land houses.*

Houses are built on stilts along the Brunei River in Bandar Seri Begawan, Brunei.

traditionally live in large longhouses near riverbanks. Each longhouse is raised on stilts and may have up to 40 rooms, with a family living in each one.

Marsh Arabs

The Ma'dan, or Marsh Arabs, live in a region of southern Iraq between the Euphrates and the Tigris (where the ancient Sumerians lived). The Ma'dan have adapted to life on the marshes, lakes, and streams between the two great rivers. They bend rows of tall, thick reeds to form arches. Then they fasten reed mats to this framework to make walls and a roof. Beside the house they build a small platform for the family's animals, mainly water buffalo. An inscribed stone found in the ancient city of Uruk suggests that the Sumerians may have lived in similar reed houses. But since 1980, the Ma'dan people's lives have changed. They have been the victims of war and persecution, and their traditional marshlands have been partly drained. Many have been forced to leave the region and give up their traditional way of life.

A village in Iraq built entirely from reeds gathered at streams and marshes.

Modern Riverside Living

In recent years, riverside locations have become very popular places to visit and live. Many riverbanks and docks have been developed or renovated, making a beautiful background for modern houses and apartments. Some of these developments have **marinas**, allowing people to moor a sailing yacht or motorboat near their home. These changes have meant that old, poor areas of cities have become new, rich ones. In cities around the world, some areas near rivers had become run down as they were used less for industry. The new trend means that these neglected areas have become very popular. Outside cities, in rural areas, there have been fewer changes.

St. Katharine's Dock

The modern marina of St. Katharine's Dock lies beside the River Thames in London, just next to Tower Bridge. It is surrounded by luxurious high-rise apartment blocks. But neither the marina nor the blocks are new. This was once a working dock, and many of the buildings were old warehouses, where goods were stored before shipping. The dock was designed and built by the famous Scottish engineer Thomas Telford (1757–1834), and it opened in 1828 to deal with goods such as tea, sugar, wool and rubber. The docks closed 140 years later and have since been redeveloped for modern living.

 New riverside apartments have been built to accommodate students at Cambridge University.

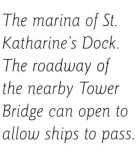

The marina of St. Katharine's Dock. The roadway of the nearby Tower Bridge can open to allow ships to pass.

At the mouth of the Tagus

At just over 1,000 kilometres long, the Tagus is the longest river on the Iberian Peninsula. Near its mouth lies the city of Lisbon, which is the capital of Portugal. A great harbour developed there during the 15th century, and many Portuguese sailors set off from there to discover distant lands around the world. Since then the river has changed course as it **silted up**, and Lisbon's waterfront was almost destroyed during a terrible earthquake in 1755. Today, the Lisbon quarter of Belém is full of museums, parks and beautiful gardens, with cafés and paths beside the river. The river is so wide here that the city has a seaside feel and is very popular with tourists.

This suspension bridge across the Tagus River in Lisbon gets very busy on weekends, when there are often traffic jams.

Farming

Water helps make land fertile, so fields beside rivers have always been popular for farming. This is another reason why people continue to live by rivers today. Farmers help nature by digging small **irrigation** channels that bring water directly to their fields from the river. On a bigger scale, **dams** and **reservoirs** help store the water needed for irrigation. In some parts of the world, such as China and India, the production of rice depends on controlling floods to irrigate river plains in the dry season. In total, nearly half the world's crops are grown on irrigated land.

Rice grows best in flooded fields; these farmers are planting rice in a paddy in Manho, Yunnan, in China.

The Yellow River

China's second longest river, the Huang He (meaning 'Yellow River'), takes its name from its muddy yellow colour. In fact, this is the muddiest river in the world. It carries a huge amount of **silt** right across China to the Gulf of Bohai. The silt makes the soil beside the banks of the river very fertile, making it excellent farmland. The ancient Chinese realized this, and their civilization began beside the Huang He, about 9,000 years ago. Today, the main crops are **cereals**, and successful use of the river's water and mud helps make

China the world's biggest producer of wheat and rice. Hundreds of millions of farming people live on the plains beside the Huang He and depend on the river for their livelihood. But they cannot depend on its waters: most years, the river runs dry at least once, and in 1997, it failed to reach the sea at all for more than 200 days. At other times, the river floods.

Imperial Valley

The people of the Nile valley use their river's water to fight the desert and irrigate their farmland, just as they have done for thousands of years. In more recent times, and in a similar way, the Imperial Valley in the United States has become one of that country's richest farming areas. Yet the valley lies in the dry Colorado Desert of southern California. It became farming land only after 1940, when the 130-kilometre long All-American Canal started taking water from the Colorado River. Many smaller irrigation channels lead off the main canal, producing fertile farming land in the desert. The main crops are alfalfa, cotton, sugar beet and melons.

About eight percent of the world's population lives along China's Huang He.

The All-American Canal is part of the irrigation system of Hoover Dam.

Fishing

Being able to catch freshwater fish was one of the main reasons why people settled beside rivers. In some parts of the world, fish became a major part of people's daily diet. Many of the native peoples of northern Russia depended on great rivers such as the Ob, Irtysh and Volga. The Nenets of northwestern Siberia traditionally fish for sturgeon and salmon. Their neighbours, the Khanti and Mansi peoples, used to hunt in the Siberian forest in winter and then return to small settlements by the rivers to fish in summer. Today, fishermen still make a living by catching valuable sturgeon near the **delta** of the River Volga, where it flows into the Caspian Sea.

The Volga still supplies one-fifth of Russia's fish catch, but large modern nets are so efficient that fewer fish now exist in the river.

Hook and line

In ancient times, people used bone hooks and traps to catch fish. They learned which parts of their rivers were best for fishing, since it was important for them to be successful. If they caught nothing, their family might have to go hungry that day. More recently, as people have found time for leisure activities, river fishing has become a fun pastime and even a serious sport.

▲ *In addition to fishing, the Nenet hunt reindeer, which are useful in making clothing and blankets.*

◄ *In most countries, children are not required to purchase fishing licences.*

Fishing for fun was mentioned in an 8th century Japanese manuscript, and in 15th-century England, a prioress named Juliana Berners wrote a book on hunting that included a chapter on 'fishing with an angle' (or rod). Today, freshwater sport fishing is popular all over the world. In order to prevent all the fish from being caught, most countries issue licences to **anglers** to fish at certain times of the year.

On the Congo

The Congo is the second longest river in Africa, after the Nile. It flows through the Democratic Republic of Congo, passing the capital, Kinshasa, on its way to the Atlantic Ocean. Many Congolese live in villages near the river, where they farm small plots of land and grow crops of cassava, maize and rice. Many of them also fish, and because large parts of the Congo River are fast and shallow, people such as the Enya (who live near Boyoma Falls) use special traps.

▲ *These fishermen use the Congo's shallow rapids to trap fish in baskets.*

21

Industrial Ports

Centuries ago, river towns on major trade routes became important ports. Many of the biggest river ports, such as Rotterdam, are very near the sea. Others are a long way inland, upstream from the sea. Around 1,500 years ago, Kiev, the capital of modern Ukraine, was a small village on the River Dnieper. When Swedish Vikings rowed and sailed down the river from the north in the ninth century, they took over the region. Kiev was a main stop on the so-called 'water road' to the city of Constantinople, and it became the capital of the first Russian state. It is still a thriving river port, yet Kiev lies 950 kilometres from the mouth of the Dnieper on the Black Sea. Another example of an inland river port is Louisville (founded in 1778), the largest city in the land-locked US state of Kentucky. It lies on the Ohio River, a tributary of the Mississippi.

The New Waterway

The Dutch city of Rotterdam lies on a branch of the River Rhine, about 30 kilometres from the North Sea. It was founded in 1328 as a small fishing village, and over the next few centuries it grew larger and attracted merchants and sailors. Then, in 1872, the Nieuwe Waterweg ('New

 The Portland Canal opened in Louisville in 1830. It was built so that ships could avoid waterfalls on the Ohio River.

The port of Rotterdam is the gateway to the inland industrial centres of northern Europe.

Waterway') canal was dug from Rotterdam to the North Sea, which meant the river port could handle much larger, ocean-going ships. In 1958, a new port (called Europoort) was built at the entrance to the canal, which handles **supertankers** that are too big to reach Rotterdam. Altogether, the giant complex is the busiest port in the world.

Manaus

The Brazilian port of Manaus lies on the River Negro, about 18 kilometres from where the river joins the Amazon. This is about 1,600 kilometres away from the mouth of the Amazon, yet ocean-going ships can reach this far inland.

Named after an Amazonian river tribe, Manaus grew from a small village in the early 20th century. Its port has floating **wharves**, which allow for seasonal changes in the depth of the river, and includes a fishing terminal. Many people have come to Manaus in search of work, and it is now a major tourist city in the heart of the Amazon rainforest, with an international airport. The city has a population of more than one million people.

The busy port of Manaus, Brazil. Cruise ships travel along the Amazon River, acting as floating hotels, just as they do on the Nile.

Controlling Rivers

People have been building dams on rivers for thousands of years. The first was probably built in ancient Egypt about 2600 BC. Ancient dams were built to control the flow of rivers and help irrigate the land. In more recent times, engineers realized that they could use the power of water to generate electricity. Today, the biggest dam in Egypt – the Aswan High Dam – produces half of the country's electricity. But it has also brought problems for farmers, because the dam stops fertile mud from moving downstream. In other parts of the world, dams have caused rivers to dry up further downstream.

▲ *The ancient Egyptians depended on the annual flood of the Nile. The Aswan High Dam was built so that the flow of the river could be spread more evenly throughout the year.*

Moving people

The Chang Jiang (meaning 'Long River') is indeed the longest river in China. It is also the site of the biggest **hydroelectric** project in the world. When it is completed in 2009, the Three Gorges Dam will be more than 2 kilometres wide and 185 metres high. Large ships will go around the dam through locks or by being lifted in a giant elevator. But the huge reservoir behind the dam will flood 19 cities and more than 300 villages. By 2002, more than 600,000 people had been

With projects such as the Three Gorges Dam, China has 10 percent of the world's potential for hydroelectric power.

▶

moved from their homes, and altogether up to two million people will have to move. An enormous project like this has created work for many Chinese people, but it will affect the daily lives of many more.

Environmental problems

The River Guadiana is 778 kilometres long – less than one-eighth the length of the Chang Jiang. The Guadiana flows through very dry parts of Spain and Portugal, and its waters are vital to

local people. In 2002, the Alqueva Dam was built on the Guadiana, and the aim is to use water stored in the dam's reservoir to irrigate very dry land in the poor Alentejo region of Portugal. This should make it easier for farmers to grow vegetables, olives and tomatoes. But at the same time the reservoir will flood villages and forests, including valuable cork oaks. It may also endanger local wildlife, such as the rare Iberian lynx. Opponents to the plan say that it has not been properly thought out or agreed with local people.

The peaceful Guadiana River flows through Portugal. The new dam is intended to help local farmers, but many fear that it will make their lives more difficult.

◀

25

Floods

People who live beside rivers face the constant threat of flooding. Almost all rivers overflow their banks from time to time. This normally happens when there has been much more rain than usual, but people often receive very little warning. Before they can do anything about it, the ground floor of their house is underwater. The Chinese call their second longest river, the Huang He, 'China's sorrow'. This is because it floods regularly and often washes houses away. They have built **embankments** to try and hold back the water, but the floodwaters are so strong that the river has changed its course many times through the centuries.

These people are fortifying the banks of the Chang Jiang before an expected heavy rainfall.

Living with Big River

The Ojibway and other Native Americans of the Great Lakes region called the waterway that flowed through their lands Mississippi, meaning 'Big River'. Since then, many villages along the Mississippi and its main tributary, the Missouri, have grown into major cities. The people who live along these rivers have learned all about floods, building high **levees** along the banks. But in 1993, the worst floods in American history left 74,000 people homeless. The whole

This railroad bridge, built in Davenport, Iowa, in 1856, was the city's only structure left untouched by Mississippi floodwaters in 1993.

state of Iowa was declared a disaster area, and in the capital city of Des Moines, the waters were more than 4 metres above flood level. Houses that were normally several miles away from the river were flooded out.

London defence

The River Thames flows right beside the Houses of Parliament and many other famous London buildings. The main threat of flooding comes from powerful surges of water from the North Sea at high tide. But today, a 520-metre wide wall of steel, that is high and strong enough to hold back floodwater, protects Londoners. The Thames Barrier has a series of gates that can be raised whenever a flood alert is issued. The gates rest on the riverbed when they are not needed so that ships can sail freely into and out of the port of London.

The steel pier roofs, which look like shells, cover the machines that open and close the gates of the Thames Barrier.

Pollution and Conservation

People make more and more demands on rivers and water resources. Unfortunately, the way in which we use rivers has led to greater water pollution. As rivers wind their way through the countryside and past farmers' fields, chemicals from fertilizers and **pesticides** are washed into the water. This is bad for fish and other river creatures, and eventually affects the water that we drink. In other areas, factories empty their waste into rivers. In cities, **sewage** may also be emptied into rivers, causing a health problem. In many parts of the world, governments are passing stricter laws to cut down on these problems and help conserve our rivers.

Holy Hindu river

The River Ganges begins in an ice cave more than 3,000 metres high up in the Himalayas. It flows for 2,510 kilometres through India and Bangladesh to the Bay of Bengal. On its way it

▲ *Varanasi is home to more than 900,000 people. Every year about one million Hindu pilgrims visit the city. They bathe in the Ganges from specially built stairways, called ghats.*

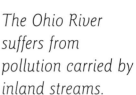

The Ohio River suffers from pollution carried by inland streams.

The Flathead River in Montana offers great white-water rafting.

passes cities such as Kanpur, Allahabad and Varanasi. The Ganges is holy to followers of the Hindu religion, who flock to Varanasi and other sacred sites to bathe in the river and cleanse themselves. The flat land that is watered by the river – known as the Gangetic Plain – is one of the most densely populated regions in the world. The river's **drainage basin** covers about a quarter of the total area of India, and more than 400 million people live there. The river's waters are vital to them, but the Ganges is being polluted by industrial waste.

Going with the flow

Rivers are increasingly used for leisure activities and sports, especially boating. Canoes, kayaks, yachts and motorboats offer great fun to people who live near rivers, as well as tourists. Many travel companies offer these activities as part of their holiday packages, in places all over the world. More serious sportspeople may take up white-water racing, a sport that developed from fishermen riding rapids. In the official sport, rivers are graded for difficulty. Canoeists, who wear life jackets and crash helmets, cover a 3-8 kilometre course as quickly as possible. There is also an Olympic version of the sport, including a slalom for pairs of canoeists who race their canoes down the wild water, steering between gate poles.

Glossary

anglers People who fish with a rod and line.

archaeologists People who study the ancient past by digging up and looking at remains.

barges Narrow, flat-bottomed boats used for carrying goods on rivers and canals.

canals Artificial waterways.

cargoes Goods carried by river (or by sea, road or air).

cereals Grasses, such as wheat, that produce grains that we can eat.

channel A deep groove carved by a river.

crops Plants, such as wheat, cotton and tobacco, grown by people.

dams Barriers built across rivers to control the flow of water.

delta The fan-shaped area at the mouth of some rivers, where the main flow splits into smaller channels.

diesel A kind of oil or petroleum used as fuel in diesel engines.

drainage basin The area of land from which rainfall runs into a particular river.

embankments Banks of earth or stone that are built to stop a river from flooding.

fertile Having rich soil and producing good crops.

gangplanks Movable footbridges leading from a riverbank to a boat.

hydroelectric To do with electric power made by the force of moving water.

Industrial Revolution The rapid development of machinery, factories and industry that began in the late 18th century.

irrigation To supply water to dry areas to help grow crops.

kayaks Kinds of canoes rowed by double-bladed paddles.

levees Another word for 'embankments'.

locks Part of a river or canal where boats can be raised or lowered to a different level.

marinas Harbours for pleasure boats.

mouth The end of a river, where it flows into the sea or into a lake.

pesticides Chemicals used to kill pests such as insects.

ports Places by rivers (or by the sea) where boats can dock, load, and unload.

rapids Part of a river where the water rushes over rocks.

reeds Kinds of tall grass plants that grow near riverbanks.

reservoirs Lakes behind dams used for storing water.

sewage Human waste matter.

silt A fine layer of mud and clay.

silted up To get clogged with mud from a river.

source The place where a river begins.

stern The back end of a boat.

supertankers Very large ships that carry oil in tanks.

tributaries Small rivers that flow into larger ones.

wharves (sing. wharf) Landing places for boats beside a river.

Index